Delicio

Healthy Instant Pot Cookbook

Cookbook

Quick and Easy Instant Pot Recipes,
Ready-to-Go Meals at Home, Your Whole Family
Will Love Every Day!

Brenda Cole

Table of Contents

CONCLUSION 117

solely under their purview. There are no scenarios in which the publisher or the original author of this work can be in any fashion deemed liable for any hardship or damages that may befall them after undertaking information described herein. Additionally, the information in the following pages is intended only for informational purposes and should thus be thought of as universal. As befitting its nature, it is presented without assurance regarding its prolonged validity or interim quality. Trademarks that are mentioned are done without written consent and can in no way be considered an endorsement from the trademark holder.

Introduction

Instant pot is a pressure cooker, also stir-fry, stew, and cook rice, cook vegetables and chicken. It's an all-in-one device, so you can season chicken and cook it in the same pan, for example. In most cases, instant pot meals can be served in less than an hour.

Cooking less time is due to the pressure cooking function that captures the steam generated by the liquid cooking environment (including liquids released from meat and vegetables), boosts the pressure and pushes the steam back.

But don't confuse with traditional pressure cookers. The instant pot, unlike the pressure cooker used by grandparents, eliminates the risk of safety with a lid that locks and remains locked until pressure is released.

Even when cooking time is over in the instant pot, you need to take an additional step-to release the pressure.

There are two ways to relieve pressure. Due to the natural pressure release, the lid valve remains in the sealing position and the pressure will naturally dissipate over time. This process takes 20 minutes to over an hour, depending on what is cooked. Low fluidity foods (such as chicken wings) take less time than high fluidity foods such as soups and marinades.

Another option is manual pressure release (also called quick release). Now you need to carefully move the valve to the ventilation position and see that the steam rises slowly and the pressure is released. This Directions is much faster, but foods with high liquid content, such as soups, take about 15 minutes to manually relieve pressure.

Which option should I use? Take into account that even if natural pressure is released, the instant pot is still under pressure. This means that the food will continue to cook while the instant pot is in sealed mode. Manual pressure relief is useful when the dishes are well cooked and need to be stopped as soon as possible.

If the goal is to prepare meals quickly, set the cooking time for dishes that are being cooked in an instant pop and release the pressure manually after the time has passed.

Instant pots (called "Instapot" by many) are one of our favorite cookware because they can handle such a wide range of foods almost easily. Instant pots range from those that work on the basics of pressure cooking to those that can be sterilized using Suicide video or some models can be controlled via Wi-Fi.

In addition, if you want to expand the range of kitchenware, the Instant Pot brand has released an air fryer that can be used to make rotisserie chicken and homemade beef jerky. There is also an independent accumulator device that can be used in instant pots to make fish, steaks and more.

The current icon instant pot works like a pressure cooker and uses heat and steam to quickly cook food. Everything from perfect carnitas to boiled eggs was cooked, but not all ingredients and DIRECTIONSs work. Here are few foods that should not be cooked in classic instant pots.

Instant pots are not pressure fryer and are not designed to handle the high temperatures required to heat cooking oils like crispy fried chicken. Of course, the instant pot is great for dishes like Carnitas, but after removing the meat from the instant pot, to get the final crispness in the meat, transfer it to a frying pan for a few minutes or to an oven top and hot Crispy in the oven.

As with slow cookers, dairy products such as cheese, milk, and sour cream will pack into instant pots using pressure cooking settings or slow cooking settings. Do not add these ingredients after the dish are cooked or create a recipe in Instapot.

There are two exceptions. One is when making yogurt. This is merely possible if you are using an instant pot recipe. The other is only when making cheesecake and following an instant pot recipe.

Although you can technically cook pasta in an instant pot, gummy may appear and cooking may be uneven. To be honest, unless you have a choice, cooking pasta in a stove pot is just as fast and easy and consistently gives you better cooked pasta.

Instead of baking the cake in an instant pot, steam it. The cake is moist-it works for things like bread pudding-but there is no good skin on the cake or on the crunchy edge everyone fights with a baked brownie. However, let's say your desire is to build a close-up or a simple dessert with your family; you can get a damp sponge in about 30 minutes, except during the DIRECTIONS time.

Canning, a technique for cooking and sealing food in a jar, is often done in a pressure cooker. Therefore, it is recommended to create a batch of jam, pickles or jelly in Instapot. Please do not.

With an instant pot, you can't monitor the temperature of what you can, like a normal pressure cooker. In canning, it is important to cook and seal the dishes correctly. Incorrect cooking and sealing can lead to the growth of bacteria that can cause food poisoning.

If you want to avoid canning in an instant pot, some newer models, such as Duo Plus, have a sterilization setting that can clean kitchen items such as baby bottles, bottles and cookware.

Instant Pot Pressure Cooker Safety Tips

Instant Pot is a very safe pressure cooker consisting of various safety mechanisms. do not worry. It will not explode immediately. Most accidents are caused by user errors and can be easily avoided. To further minimize the possibility of an accident, we have compiled a list of safety tips.

1 Don't leave it alone

It is not recommended to leave home while cooking an instant pot. If you have to leave it alone, make sure it is under pressure and no steam is coming out.

2 Do not use KFC in instant pot

Do not fry in an instant pot or other pressure cooker.

KFC uses a commercial pressure fryer specially made to fry chicken (the latest one that operates at 5 PSI). Instant pots (10.5-11.6 PSI) are specially made to make our lives easier.

3 water intake!

Instant pots require a minimum of 1 1/2 cup liquid (Instant Pot Official Number) 1 cup liquid to reach and maintain pressure.

The liquid can be a combination of gravy, vinegar, water, chicken etc.

4 half full or half empty

The max line printed on the inner pot of the instant pot is not for pressure cooking.

For pressure cooking: up to 2/3 full

Food for pressure cooking that expands during cooking (grains, beans, dried vegetables, etc.): up to 1/2

5 Not a facial steamer

Deep cleaning is not performed even if the pressure cooker steam is used once.

When opening, always tilt the lid away from you. Wear waterproof and heat-resistant silicone gloves especially when performing quick release.

6 never use power

In situations of zero, you should try to force open the lid of the instant pot pressure cooker, unless you want to prevent a light saber from hitting your face.

7 Wash Up & Checkout

If you want to be secured, wash the lid after each use and clean the anti-block shield and inner pot. Make sure that the gasket (silicon seal ring) is in good shape and that there is no food residue in the anti-block shield before use.

Usually silicone seal rings should be replaced every 18-24 months. It is always advisable to keep extra things.

Do not purchase a sealing ring from a third party because it is an integral part of the safety features of the instant ring. Using sealing rings that have not been tested with instant pot products can create serious safety concerns."

Before use, make sure that the sealing ring is securely fixed to the sealing ring rack and the anti-block shield is properly attached to the vapor discharge pipe.

A properly fitted sealing ring can be moved clockwise or counterclockwise in the sealing ring rack with little force.

With instant pots, the whole family can cook meals in less than 30 minutes. Cooked dishes such as rice, chicken, beef stew, sauce, yakitori can be cooked for 30-60 minutes from the beginning to the end. And yes, you can bake bread in an instant pot.

Old and ketogenic diet fans love instant pots for their ability to `` roast '' meat in such a short time, but vegetarians and vegans that can quickly cook dishes such as pumpkin soup, baked potatoes and marinated potato chilis, also highly appreciated oatmeal cream and macaroni and cheese.

Even dried beans, which usually require overnight cooking, can be prepared in 30 minutes to make spicy hummus.

Duck with Sticky Cranberry Sauce

Preparation Time: 10 minutes

Cooking Time: 25 minutes

Servings: 6

Ingredients:

3 pounds whole duck

Kosher salt, to taste

1/2 teaspoon freshly ground black pepper

1/2 teaspoon red pepper flakes

1/2 teaspoon smoked paprika

1 teaspoon onion powder

2 cloves garlic, minced

1 cup chicken stock

1 tablespoon butter

1/2 cup cranberries, halved

1 tablespoon brown sugar

1/4 cup raspberry vinegar

1 teaspoon wholegrain mustard

Directions:

Press the "Sauté" button and melt the butter; place the duck skin-side down in the inner pot and sear until the skin is crisp and brown. Flip and cook for another 4 minutes.

Disregard all but a tablespoon of the fat. Add the salt, black pepper, red pepper, paprika, onion powder, garlic, and chicken stock to the inner pot.

Secure the lid. Choose the "Manual" mode and cook for 25 minutes at High pressure. Once done coooking, use a natural pressure release; carefully remove the lid.

Now, remove the duck from the inner pot.

Press the "Sauté" button and add the remaining ingredients to the cooking liquid.

Continue to cook for 5 to 6 minutes, until the cranberries start to slightly break down and soften. Spoon over the reserved duck and serve immediately. Bon appétit!

Nutrition:

Calories – 517

Protein – 40.6 g.

Fat – 36.7 g.

Carbs – 3.3 g.

Asian Ginger-Glazed Duck Breast

Preparation Time: 5 minutes

Cooking Time: 20 minutes

Servings: 4

Ingredients:

1 teaspoon sesame oil

2 pounds duck breasts

Sea salt and black pepper, to taste

1 teaspoon red pepper flakes

1 teaspoon dry mustard

1 tablespoon paprika

1 teaspoon ground star anise

1 teaspoon ground ginger

1 cup chicken broth

Ginger Glaze:

1 tablespoon peanut oil

1-inch piece ginger, finely chopped

3 cloves garlic, finely chopped

1 tablespoon Sriracha sauce

1/4 cup low-sodium soy sauce

1/4 cup honey

Directions:

Press the "Sauté" button to preheat your Instant Pot.

Heat the sesame seed oil and sear the duck breasts for 5 minutes, stirring periodically. Sprinkle your spices all over the duck breasts. Add the chicken broth.

Make sure to lock the lid and choose the "Poultry" mode. Cook for 15 minutes. Afterwards, use a quick release and carefully remove the lid. Remove the duck breasts from the inner pot.

After that, stir in the other ingredients for the ginger glaze; stir well to combine.

Press the "Sauté" button to preheat your Instant Pot. Cook until thoroughly heated. Place the duck breasts in the serving plates and brush with the ginger glaze. Serve warm and enjoy!

Nutrition:

Calories – 411

Protein – 47.6 g.

Fat – 14.5 g.

Carbs – 22.1 g.

Xiang Su Ya (Szechuan Duck)

Preparation Time: 10 minutes

Cooking Time: 25 minutes

Servings: 6

Ingredients:

2 tablespoons Szechuan peppercorns

1 teaspoon Chinese 5-spice powder

2 tablespoons salt

3 pounds whole duck

4 cloves garlic, sliced

2 star anise

1/4 cup soy sauce

1/4 cup Shaoxing rice wine

1 red chili pepper, chopped

1 tablespoon dark brown sugar

1 cup water

Directions:

Press the "Sauté" button to preheat your Instant Pot. Then, add the Szechuan peppercorn to the inner pot and roast until really fragrant. Remove it to a spice grinder and ground into a powder.

Add the Chinese 5-spice powder and salt. Rub the duck with the spice mixture. Leave it to marinate overnight.

Press the "Sauté" button to preheat your Instant Pot. Now, place the duck skin-side down in the inner pot and sear until the skin is crisp and brown. Flip and cook for 4 to 5 minutes more.

Stir in the other ingredients.

Make sure to lock the lid and choose the "Manual" mode. Cook for 25 minutes at High pressure. Afterwards, use a quick release and carefully remove the lid. Serve warm.

Nutrition:

Calories – 525

Protein – 40.5 g.

Fat – 37.2 g.

Carbs – 4.5 g.

Braised Duck with Mixed Vegetables

Preparation Time: 10 minutes

Cooking Time: 20 minutes

Servings: 4

Ingredients:

2 pounds whole duck

1 cup chicken stock

1 teaspoon smoked paprika

1 bay leaf

1 tablespoon butter, melted

1 onion, quartered

1 red bell pepper, deseeded and sliced

1 green bell pepper, deseeded and sliced

Kosher salt and black pepper, to taste

2 carrots, sliced

1 celery stalk, sliced

4 cloves garlic, sliced

2 rosemary sprigs

1 thyme sprig

2 tablespoons balsamic vinegar

2 tablespoons Worcestershire sauce

Directions:

Press the "Sauté" button to preheat your Instant Pot. Now, place the duck skin-side down in the inner pot and sear until the skin is crisp and brown. Flip and cook for 4 to 5 minutes more.

Add the chicken stock, salt, black pepper, smoked paprika, and bay leaf to the inner pot.

Make sure to lock the lid and choose the "Manual" mode. Cook for 20 minutes at High pressure. Afterwards, use a quick release and carefully remove the lid.

Add the remaining ingredients in the order listed above. Secure the lid. Choose the "Manual" mode and cook for 3 minutes at High pressure. Once done cooking, use a quick pressure release; carefully remove the lid. Serve immediately.

Nutrition:

Calories – 554

Protein – 41.9 g.

Fat – 38 g.

Carbs – 9.3 g.

Aromatic Duck Salad

Preparation Time: 5 minutes

Cooking Time: 20 minutes

Servings: 6

Ingredients:

3 pounds duck breasts

1 cup water

2 heads romaine lettuce, cut into pieces

Salt and black pepper, to taste

2 tomatoes, diced

2 red onions, sliced diagonally

2 tablespoons balsamic vinegar

1 garlic clove, minced

1 teaspoon fresh ginger, grated

2 tablespoons tamari sauce

2 tablespoons peanut butter

Directions:

Put the duck breasts and water into the inner pot.

Make sure to lock the lid and choose the "Poultry" mode.

Cook for 15 minutes at High pressure. Afterwards, use a quick release and carefully remove the lid.

Now, slice the meat into strips and place in a salad bowl. Season with salt and pepper. Add the romaine lettuce, tomatoes, and onion.

In a small mixing dish, whisk the balsamic vinegar, garlic, ginger, tamari sauce, and peanut butter. Dress the salad and serve well chilled. Bon appétit!

Nutrition:

Calories – 349

Protein – 48.6 g.

Fat – 11.3 g.

Carbs – 12.3 g.

Duck with Hoisin Sauce

Preparation Time: 10 minutes

Cooking Time: 30 minutes

Servings: 6

Ingredients:

3 pounds whole duck

Salt and ground black pepper, to taste

1 cup roasted vegetable broth

2 carrots, chopped

1 head broccoli, chopped into florets

1 leek, white part only, chopped

1 small bunch of fresh coriander stalks, roughly chopped

2 cloves garlic, sliced

1 bay leaf

1/2 cup Hoisin sauce

1 lemon, cut into wedges

Directions:

Press the "Sauté" button to preheat your Instant Pot.
Now, cook the duck for 4 to 5 minutes or until the skin
turns golden brown. Pour in the roasted vegetable broth.
Make sure to lock the lid and choose the "Manual" mode.
Cook for 25 minutes at High pressure. Afterwards, use a
quick release and carefully remove the lid.

Add the vegetables, coriander, garlic, and bay leaf.

Secure the lid. Choose the "Manual" mode and cook for 3 minutes at High pressure. Once done cooking, use a quick pressure release; carefully remove the lid.

Take the duck to a chopping board and rest for 5 minutes before cutting and serving.

Lastly, slice the duck and serve with the braised vegetables, Hoisin sauce, and lemon wedges. Bon appétit!

Nutrition:

Calories – 385

Protein – 43.8 g.

Fat – 14.6 g.

Carbs – 17.5 g.

Japanese Duck and Rice Bowl

Preparation Time: 5 minutes

Cooking Time: 15 minutes

Servings: 4

Ingredients:

2 pounds duck breasts, skinless and boneless

2 tablespoons orange juice

2 tablespoons Mirin

2 tablespoons tamari

1 tablespoon sesame oil

1 cup vegetable broth

Sea salt and fresh pepper, to taste

2 garlic cloves, grated

1 teaspoon honey

1 shallot, chopped

1/4 cup fresh parsley leaves,

1 fresh lemon, juiced

2 tablespoons extra-virgin oil

1 cup Chinese cabbage, shredded

2 tablespoons sesame seeds, toasted

1 red chili, finely chopped

2 cups cooked rice

1 tablespoon olive oil

4 eggs

Directions:

Place the duck breasts, orange juice, Mirin, and tamari sauce in a ceramic dish. Let it marinate for 1 hour in your refrigerator.

Press the "Sauté" button and heat the oil until sizzling. Cook the duck for about 5 minutes or until it is no longer pink.

Add the vegetable broth and secure the lid.

Pick the "Manual" mode and cook for 10 minutes at High pressure. Once done coooking,use a quick pressure release; carefully remove the lid.

Slice the duck and transfer to a nice serving bowl. Add the garlic, honey, salt, black pepper, shallot, fresh parsley, lemon, oil, cabbage, sesame seeds, chili pepper, and cooked rice.

Heat the olive oil in a pan over medium-high flame. Fry the eggs until the whites are completely set. Put the eggs on top and serve immediately.

Nutrition:

Calories – 631

Protein – 56.6 g.

Fat – 31.2 g.

Carbs – 28.8 g.

Sweet Chicken Carnitas in Lettuce Wraps

Preparation Time: 10 minutes

Cooking Time: 40 minutes

Servings: 6

Ingredients:

2 tbsp canola oil

2 lb chicken thighs, boneless, skinless

1 cup pineapple juice

1/3 cup water

¼ cup soy sauce

2 tbsp maple syrup

1 tbsp rice vinegar

1 tsp chili-garlic sauce

3 tbsp cornstarch

Salt and black pepper to taste

2 cups canned pinto beans, rinsed

12 lettuce large leaves

Directions:

Warm oil on Sauté. In batches, stir chicken in the oil for 5 minutes until browned. Set aside in a bowl.

Into your pot, mix chili-garlic sauce, pineapple juice, soy sauce, vinegar, maple syrup, and water; Stir in chicken to coat.

Make sure to lock the lid and cook on High Pressure for 7 minutes. Release Pressure naturally for 10 minutes. Shred the chicken with two forks. Take ¼ cup liquid from the pot to a bowl; Stir in cornstarch to dissolve.

Mix the cornstarch mixture with the mixture in the pot and return the chicken. Choose Sauté and cook for 5 minutes until the sauce thickens; add pepper and salt for seasoning. Transfer beans into lettuce leaves, top with chicken carnitas and serve.

Nutrition:

Calories – 675

Protein – 52 g.

Fat – 36.5 g.

Carbs – 14.8 g.

Salsa Verde Chicken

Preparation Time: 5 minutes

Cooking Time: 12 minutes

Servings: 4

Ingredients:

Salt – 1 tsp.

Chili powder – 1 tsp.

Garlic powder – ½ tsp.

Chicken breasts – 2 (6-ounce) boneless, skinless

Coconut oil – 1 Tbsp.

Chicken broth – ¼ cup

Salsa Verde – 1 cup

Butter – 2 Tbsp.

Directions:

In a bowl, mix all the seasoning and rub the chicken with it.

Press the Sauté and add coconut oil.

Place the chicken and sear 3 to 4 minutes on each side.

Add salsa verde and chicken broth.

Make sure to lock the lid and press Manual. Cook 12 minutes on High.

Use a natural release and open the lid.

Remove the chicken and shred with forks.

Return chicken to the warm pot and add butter.

Allow to melt for 10 minutes.

Serve warm with toppings.

Nutrition:

Calories – 185

Protein – 20.2 g.

Fat – 13.4 g.

Carbs – 2.8 g.

Ranch Chicken

Preparation Time: 5 minutes

Cooking Time: 20 minutes

Servings: 6

Ingredients:

Salt – 1 tsp.

Pepper – ¼ tsp.

Dried oregano – ¼ tsp.

Garlic powder – ½ tsp.

Skinless chicken breasts – 3 (6-ounce)

Chicken broth – 1 cup

Dry ranch – 1 packet

Cream cheese – 8 ounces

Butter – 1 stick

Directions:

In a bowl, mix the seasoning and rub the chicken with it.

Place the chicken into the Instant Pot and add broth.

Place butter and cream cheese on top of the chicken.

Make sure to lock the lid and cook for20 minutes on High.

Do a natural release.

Remove chicken and shred with forks.

Return to Instant Pot and serve.

Nutrition:

Calories – 383

Protein – 21.9 g.

Fat – 26.9 g.

Carbs – 4.5 g.

Lemon Herb Whole Chicken

Preparation Time: 5 minutes

Cooking Time: 25 minutes

Servings: 4

Ingredients:

Salt – 3 tsp.

Garlic powder – 3 tsp.

Dried rosemary – 2 tsp.

Dried parsley – 2 tsp.

Pepper – 1 tsp.

Whole chicken – 1 (5 pound)

Coconut oil – 2 Tbsp.

Chicken Broth – 1 cup

Lemon – 1, zested and quartered

Directions:

In a bowl, mix pepper, parsley, rosemary, garlic, and salt.

Rub the chicken with the mixture.

Press Sauté and add oil to the Instant Pot.

Add chicken and brown for 5 to 7 minutes.

Press Cancel and remove the chicken.

Add broth and deglaze the pot.

Place lemon quarters inside the chicken and sprinkle the chicken with lemon zest.

Place chicken back into the pot.

Make sure to lock the lid and press Meat.

Cook on High for 25 minutes.

Do a natural release when done.

Slice the chicken and serve.

Nutrition:

Calories – 861

Protein – 45.5 g.

Fat – 62.9 g.

Carbs – 2.1 g.

Sweet and Sour Meatballs

Preparation Time: 10 minutes

Cooking Time: 10 minutes

Servings: 4

Ingredients:

Ground chicken – 1 pound

Egg – 1

Salt – 1 tsp.

Pepper – 1 tsp.

Garlic powder – 1 tsp.

Diced onion – ½

Water – 1

Erythritol – 2 tsp.

Rice vinegar – 1 tsp.

No sugar added ketchup – 2 tsp.

Sriracha – ½ tsp.

Directions:

In a bowl, mix onion, garlic powder, salt, pepper, egg, and chicken.

Make small balls with the mixture.

Add water to the Instant Pot.

Place meatballs on the steam rack.

Make sure to lock the lid and press Manual.

Cook 10 minutes on High.

In a bowl, mix sriracha, ketchup, vinegar, and erythritol.

When finished, do a quick release.

Toss meatballs in the sauce.

Serve.

Nutrition:

Calories – 152

Protein – 17.4 g.

Fat – 7.6 g.

Carbs – 1.7 g.

Pesto Chicken

Preparation Time: 5 minutes

Cooking Time: 20 minutes

Servings: 2

Ingredients:

Boneless, skinless chicken breasts – 2 (6-oz.) butterflied

Salt – ½ tsp.

Pepper – ¼ tsp.

Garlic powder – ¼ tsp.

Dried parsley – ¼ tsp.

Coconut oil – 2 Tbsp.

Water – 1 cup

Whole-milk ricotta – ¼ cup

Pesto – ¼ cup

Shredded whole-milk mozzarella cheese – ¼ cup

Chopped parsley for garnish

Directions:

Rub the chicken with seasonings.

Melt the oil in the instant Pot on Sauté.

Add chicken and sauté for 3 to 5 minutes.

Remove chicken and place in a bowl.

Pour water into the pot and deglaze.

Add the ricotta onto the chicken.

Pour pesto and drizzle with mozzarella.

Cover the dish with foil.

Place a steam rack into the Instant Pot and place the foil covered dish on top.

Cover with the lid and press Manual.

Cook 20 minutes on High.

Do a natural release when done.

Serve.

Nutrition:

Calories – 518

Protein – 46.5 g.

Fat – 31.8 g.

Carbs – 3.6 g.

Chicken Piccata

Preparation Time: 5 minutes

Cooking Time: 20 minutes

Servings: 4

Ingredients:

Boneless, skinless chicken breasts – 4 (6-oz.)

Salt – ½ tsp.

Pepper – ¼ tsp.

Garlic powder – ½ tsp.

Coconut oil – 2 Tbsp.

Water – 1 cup

Butter – 4 Tbsp.

Juice of 1 lemon

Capers – 2 Tbsp.

Garlic – 2 cloves, minced

Xanthan gum – ¼ tsp.

Directions:

Rub the chicken with garlic powder, pepper, and salt.

Melt the oil on Sauté in the Instant Pot.

Cook the chicken until golden on each side.

Remove chicken and add water to deglaze the pot.

Place the steam rack and add the chicken.

Make sure to lock the lid and press Manual.

Cook for 10 minutes on High.

Do a natural release when done.

Remove chicken and set aside.

Strain the broth in a bowl and then return to the Instant Pot.

Press Sauté and add, butter, xanthan gum, garlic, capers, and lemon juice.

Stir continuously until the sauce thickens, about 5 minutes.

Serve over chicken.

Nutrition:

Calories – 337

Protein – 32.3 g.

Fat – 19.5 g.

Carbs – 1.4 g.

Garlic Parmesan Drumsticks

Preparation Time: 5 minutes

Cooking Time: 15 minutes

Servings: 4

Ingredients:

Chicken drumsticks – 2 pounds (about 8 pieces)

Salt – 1 tsp.

Pepper – ¼ tsp.

Garlic powder – ½ tsp.

Dried parsley – 1 tsp.

Dried oregano – ½ tsp.

Water – 1 cup

Butter – 1 stick

Chicken broth – ½ cup

Grated Parmesan cheese – ½ cup

Cream cheese – 2 ounces, softened

Heavy cream – ¼ cup

Pepper – 1/8 tsp.

Directions:

Rub the drumsticks with the seasoning.

Pour the water to the Instant Pot and place steam rack.

Place drumsticks on top and close the lid.

Press Manual and cook 15 minutes on High.

Do a natural release and open.

If you want crispy skin, then broil the chicken in a preheated oven for 3 to 5 minutes per side.

Meanwhile, pour water into the Instant Pot and press Sauté.

Melt the butter and add pepper, heavy cream, cream cheese, Parmesan, and broth.

Whisk to mix.

Pour the sauce over drumsticks.

Garnish with parsley and serve.

Nutrition:

Calories – 786

Protein – 53.3 g.

Fat – 55.4 g.

Carbs – 3.4 g.

Chicken Enchilada Bowl

Preparation Time: 10 minutes

Cooking Time: 25 minutes

Servings: 4

Ingredients:

Boneless, skinless chicken breasts – 2 (6-ounce)

Salt – ½ tsp.

Garlic powder – ½ tsp.

Pepper – ¼ tsp.

Chili powder – 2 tsp.

Coconut oil – 2 Tbsp.

Red enchilada sauce – ¾ cup

Chicken broth – ¼ cup

Diced onion – ¼ cup

Green chilies -1 (4-ounce) can

Cooked cauliflower rice – 2 cups

Diced avocado – 1

Sour cream – ½ cup

Shredded cheddar cheese – 1 cup

Directions:

Rub chicken with chili powder, pepper, garlic powder, and salt.

Press Sauté and melt the oil into the Instant Pot.

Sear the chicken on both sides and press Cancel.

Add broth and sauce.

Add chilies and onions to the pot and close the lid.

Press Manual and cook 25 minutes on High.

Do a quick release and shred chicken.

Serve chicken over cauliflower rice top with cheddar, sour cream, and avocado.

Nutrition:

Calories – 425

Protein – 29.4 g.

Fat – 26 g.

Carbs – 7.1 g.

Turkey Tomato Meatballs

Preparation Time: 10 minutes

Cooking Time: 10 minutes

Servings: 4

Ingredients:

Almond flour – 1/3 cup

Diced tomatoes – 3 ½ cups

Basil – 1 tsp.

Ground turkey – 1 pound

Chicken stock – ¼ cup

Onion – ¼, diced

Minced garlic – 1 tsp.

Italian seasoning – 1 tsp.

Salt and black pepper to taste

Directions:

In a bowl, place the flour, onion, basil, and turkey. Season with salt and pepper.

Mix and make meatballs.

Add the meatballs and other ingredients into the Instant Pot and stir to mix well.

Make sure to lock the lid and press Manual.

Cook 10 minutes on High.

Do a quick release when done.

Open the lid and serve.

Nutrition:

Calories – 326

Protein – 27 g.

Fat – 14 g.

Carbs – 4 g.

Cauliflower Turkey Salsa

Preparation Time: 10 minutes

Cooking Time: 15 minutes

Servings: 5

Ingredients:

Cooked and shredded turkey – 2 cups

Cream cheese – 4 ounces

Cauliflower florets – 2 ½ cups, chopped

Shredded cheddar cheese – 1 cup

Sour cream – ¼ cup

Salsa verde – ½ cup

Salt and ground black pepper to taste

Water – 1 ½ cups

Dircctions:

Add water to the Instant Pot.

Grease a steamer basket with oil and place in the pot.

Arrange the ingredients over the basket and mix.

Make sure to lock the lid and press Manual.

Cook 15 minutes on High.

Do a quick release when done.

Open the lid and serve.

Nutrition:

Calories – 324

Protein – 34 g.

Fat – 18 g.

Carbs – 5 g.

Barbecue Wings

Preparation Time: 5 minutes

Cooking Time: 12 minutes

Servings: 4

Ingredients:

Chicken wings 1 pound

Salt – 1 tsp.

Pepper ½ tsp.

Garlic powder – ¼ tsp.

Sugar-free barbecue sauce – 1 cup, divided

Water – 1 cup

Directions:

In a bowl, mix wings, half of the sauce, garlic powder, salt, and pepper.

Add water into the Instant Pot and place a steam rack.

Place wings on the steam rack and close the lid.

Press Manual and cook 12 minutes on High.

Do a quick release, remove and toss in remaining sauce.

If you want crispier wings, then broil the wings for 5 to 7 minutes in the oven.

Nutrition:

Calories – 237,Protein – 19.9 g., Fat – 14.9 g.

Carbs – 4.2 g.

Jamaican Curry Chicken

Preparation Time: 5 minutes

Cooking Time: 20 minutes

Servings: 4

Ingredients:

Chicken drumsticks – 1 ½ pound

Salt – 1 tsp.

Jamaican curry powder – 1 Tbsp.

Onion – ½, diced

Dried thyme – ½ tsp.

Chicken broth – 1 cup

Directions:

Rub the drumsticks with salt and curry powder.

Place rest of the ingredients and chicken into the Instant Pot.

Press Manual and cook 20 minutes on High.

Do a natural release and serve.

Nutrition:

Calories – 284

Protein – 31.3 g.

Fat – 14.11 g.

Carbs – 1.4 g.

Chicken Parmesan

Preparation Time: 5 minutes

Cooking Time: 15 minutes

Servings: 2

Ingredients:

Coconut oil – 2 Tbsp.

Salt – ½ tsp.

Pepper – ¼ tsp.

Dried basil – ¼ tsp.

Garlic powder – ½ tsp.

Dried parsley – ¼ tsp.

Boneless, skinless chicken breasts – 2 (6-ounce), butterflied

Water – ½ cup

No sugar added tomato sauce – 1 cup

Grated Parmesan cheese – ¼ cup

Shredded whole-milk mozzarella cheese – ¼ cup

Directions:

Melt the oil in the Instant Pot on Sauté.

Rub the chicken with seasoning and sear 4 minutes on each side.

Add tomato sauce and water and close the lid.

Press Manual and cook 15 minutes on High.

When done, do a quick release befoere opening.

Add mozzarella and Parmesan and place the lid.

Keep the pot on Keep Warm mode for 5 minutes.

Top with parsley and serve.

Nutrition:

Calories – 548

Protein – 48.9 g.

Fat – 28.7 g.

Carbs – 8.4 g.

Italian Chicken Thighs

Preparation Time: 10 minutes

Cooking Time: 15 minutes

Servings: 4

Ingredients:

Chicken thighs – 4 (bone-in)

Garlic – 2 cloves, minced

Salt – 1 tsp.

Pepper – ¼ tsp.

Dried basil – ¼ tsp.

Dried parsley – ¼ tsp.

Dried oregano – ½ tsp.

Water – 1 cup

Directions:

Place chicken in a bowl.

Rub the chicken with all the spices, herbs, and seasoning.

Put water in the Instant Pot and place steam rack.

Place chicken thighs on the steam rack and close the lid.

Press Manual and cook 15 minutes on High.

Do a quick release and remove.

Broil chicken in the oven for 3 to 5 minutes if you want crispy chicken.

Nutrition:

Calories – 429

Protein – 32 g.

Fat – 28.8 g.

Carbs – 1 g.

Mediterranean Chicken Bowl with Pine Nuts

Preparation Time: 10 minutes

Cooking Time: 20 minutes

Servings: 4

Ingredients:

Chicken legs – 1 pound, skinless and cut into pieces

Olive oil – 1 Tbsp.

Red wine vinegar – 2 Tbsp.

Watercress – 1 ounce, tough stalks removed and chopped

Bell pepper – 1, chopped

Sweet onion – 1, sliced

Garlic – 2 cloves, minced

Cucumber – 1, sliced

Gem lettuce – 2 cups, leaves separated

Ground black pepper and salt to taste

Spanish paprika – 1 tsp.

Marjoram – ½ tsp.

Oregano – ½ tsp.

Pine nuts – 4 Tbsp.

Water – 1 cup, for the pot

Directions:

Add 1 cup water and metal rack to the Instant Pot. Lower the chicken legs onto the metal rack.

Cover and cook on Steam mode for 15 minutes on High. Do a quick release and open.

Slice the chicken into bite-sized pieces and discard the bones. Place the meat into a bowl.

Clean the Instant Pot and add 1 tbsp. oil. Heat on Sauté.

Add sweet onion and garlic and sauté for 5 minutes. Add remaining ingredients excluding the pine nuts and lettuce and mix.

Add the mixture to the bowl and toss to combine.

Garnish with pine nuts and serve with lettuce leaves.

Nutrition:

Calories – 328

Protein – 24.7 g.

Fat – 20.6 g.

Carbs – 11.1 g.

Chicken with Mustard Greens and Olives

Preparation Time: 5 minutes

Cooking Time: 15 minutes

Servings: 4

Ingredients:

Boneless chicken thighs – 4

Mustard greens – 1 bunch, rinsed and chopped

Green olives – ½ cup, pitted

Cherry tomatoes – ½ cup, washed

Minced garlic – 1 ½ tsp.

Salt – ¾ tsp.

Ground black pepper – ½ tsp.

Honey – 1 tsp.

Dijon mustard – 1 tsp.

Olive oil – 4 Tbsp.

Lemon – 1, juiced

White wine – 1 cup

Directions:

Add the oil to the Instant Pot.

Season chicken with salt, black pepper. Put the chicken in the Instant Pot along with mustard greens, garlic, olives, tomatoes, mustard, and honey.

Add the lemon juice and wine and close the lid.

Cook on High for 15 minutes. Do a quick release and open. Serve.

Nutrition:

Calories – 336.5

Protein – 26.9 g.

Fat – 23.5 g.

Carbs – 4.2 g.

Greek Chicken and Rice

Preparation Time: 10 minutes

Cooking Time: 4 minutes

Servings: 4

Ingredients:

Rice – 1 cup

Chicken breasts – 3, diced

Red bell pepper – 1, chopped

Yellow bell pepper – 1, chopped

Zucchini – 1, sliced

Red onion – 1, chopped

Minced garlic – 2 tsp.

Salt – ½ tsp.

Ground black pepper – ½ tsp.

Oregano – 1 Tbsp.

Lemon juice – 3 Tbsp.

Olive oil – 2 Tbsp.

Chicken broth – 1 ½ cups

Parsley – ¼ cup, chopped

Feta cheese – ¼ cup, crumbled

Directions:

Add everything in the Instant Pot except for zucchini, peppers, cheese, and parsley.

Mix and cover the pot. Cook 4 minutes on High.

Do a natural release and open. Stir in chicken and remaining ingredients.

Close and let rest for 10 minutes.

Top with cheese and serve.

Nutrition:

Calories – 314.3

Protein – 26.7 g.

Fat – 9 g.

Carbs – 31.4 g.

Maple Mustard Turkey Thighs

Preparation Time: 10 minutes

Cooking Time: 30 minutes

Servings: 4

Ingredients:

Turkey thighs – 2 (3 lb.) bone-in, skin on

Olive oil – ½ cup

Fresh rosemary – 1 tsp. chopped

Fresh thyme – 1 tsp. chopped

Smoked paprika – 1 Tbsp.

Dijon mustard – 2 Tbsp.

Maple syrup – ½ cup

Onion – 1, chopped

Celery – 5 stalks, chopped

Carrots – 5, chopped

Rosemary – 4 sprigs

Thyme – 2 sprigs

Salt – 1 tsp.

Pepper – ½ tsp.

Water – 1 cup

Directions:

Add the oil, thyme, rosemary, maple syrup, smoked paprika, and Dijon mustard to the Instant Pot.

Cook the mixture on Sauté and stir occasionally.

Add the salt, pepper, and half the maple syrup mixture to the turkey thighs. Mix.

Add the water, celery, onion, rosemary, thyme, and carrots to the Instant Pot.

Place the trivet in the pot. Then place turkey thighs over the trivet.

Pour the remaining maple syrup mixture over the thighs.

Cover. Cook on High for 30 minutes. Then do a natural release.

Remove the lid, then take out the turkey thighs.

Cut them into slices, pour maple mustard mixture over the sliced thighs and serve.

Nutrition:

Calories – 633

Protein – 44 g.

Fat – 34 g.

Carbs – 41 g.

Turkey Cheese Gnocchi

Preparation Time: 10 minutes

Cooking Time: 25 minutes

Servings: 6

Ingredients:

Turkey boneless pieces – 1 pound

Fresh spinach – 2 cups, chopped

Mozzarella cheese – 2 cups, shredded

Parmesan cheese – ½ cup, shredded

Olive oil – 2 Tbsp.

Black pepper – ½ tsp.

Shallots – ¼ cup, chopped

Garlic minced – 2 cloves

Sun-dried tomatoes – ¼ cup, chopped

Cream – 1 cup

Chicken broth – 2 cups

Gnocchi – 2 lbs.

Salt – ½ tsp.

Directions:

Press Saute and then add the oil.

Add the turkey with salt and pepper. Cook 3 minutes on each side.

Add the garlic, tomatoes, and shallots to the pot. Cook and stir for 2 minutes.

Add the cream and chicken broth to the pot. Cover the pot.

Cook on High for 10 minutes, then do a natural release.

Add gnocchi to the mixture and press Sauté. Cook 5 minutes, or until gnocchi is tender.

Add cheese and serve.

Nutrition:

Calories – 1033

Protein – 99.2 g.

Fat – 19.9 g.

Carbs – 32.6 g.

Delicious Orange Spice Chicken

Preparation Time: 10 minutes

Cooking Time: 15 minutes

Servings: 6

Ingredients:

Chicken breast – 2 lb. chopped

Olive oil – 2 Tbsp.

Garlic – 2 heads, minced

Granulated sugar – ¼ cup

Brown sugar – ¼ cup

Soy sauce – ¼ cup

Tomato sauce – 1 cup

Orange juice – 1 cup

Corn starch – 4 Tbsp.

Green onions – 4, chopped

Orange zest – 2 Tbsp.

Salt and pepper to taste

Directions:

Add oil and press Sauté.

Put the chicken in and cook for 3 minutes.

Then add the rest of the ingredients to the pot, except for the corn starch, orange juice, green onions, and orange zest. Mix and cover.

Cook 7 minutes on Poultry on High.

Do a natural release and open.

Mix corn-starch with orange juice in a bowl and add to the pot.

Press Sauté and cook the chicken in the sauce for 5 minutes. Stir constantly until it thickens.

Garnish with chopped green onions and orange zest and serve.

Nutrition:

Calories – 818

Protein – 128.2 g.

Fat – 19.6 g.

Carbs – 23.7 g.

Chicken with Smoked Paprika

Preparation Time: 10 minutes

Cooking Time: 20 minutes

Servings: 6

Ingredients:

Chicken breasts – 1 ½ lb. cut into small pieces

Smoked paprika – 2 tsp.

Olive oil – 1 tsp.

Bacon – 3 strips, chopped

Onion – 1, chopped

Garlic – 2 cloves, minced

Red bell pepper – 1, chopped

Salt – ½ tsp.

Beer – 1 (12 oz.) can

White rice – 1 cup

Bacon – 2 strips, cooked (topping)

Dircctions:

Add the oil and bacon in the pot. Sauté for 3 minutes.

Add the bell pepper and stir-fry for 3 minutes more.

Add chopped onion and cook for 2 minutes.

Put in the garlic and cook for 1 minute.

Add all the seasoning to the pot and add the beer. Mix.

Add the chicken and rice and cover the pot.

Cook on High for 10 minutes. Do a quick release and open.

Serve dish topped with bacon.

Nutrition:

Calories – 524

Protein – 68.5 g.

Fat – 10.3 g.

Carbs – 29.3 g.

Green Chili Adobo Chicken

Preparation Time: 10 minutes

Cooking Time: 25 minutes

Servings: 6

Ingredients:

Boneless, skinless chicken breasts – 6

Adobo all-purpose seasoning with pepper – 1 Tbsp.

Diced tomatoes – 2 cups

Water – ½ cup

Turmeric – 1 Tbsp.

Diced green chilies – 1 cup

Directions:

Place the chicken breasts to the Instant Pot.

Add seasoning pepper to the chicken and sprinkle on both sides.

Add sliced tomatoes to the chicken.

Pour half cup of water over the chicken.

Cover and cook on High for 25 minutes.

Do a natural release and open.

Shred the chicken and serve.

Nutrition:

Calories – 204,Protein – 32.9 g., Fat – 4.2 g.

Carbs – 7.6 g.

Turkey Noodle Soup

Preparation Time: 10 minutes

Cooking Time: 40 minutes

Servings: 4

Ingredients:

Shredded turkey – 1 cup

Turkey carcass – 1, leftover from a carved turkey

Water – 14 cups

Onion – 1, chopped

Carrots -3, chopped

Celery – 2 stalks, chopped

Salt and pepper to taste

Soup

Cooked turkey meat – 3 cups, chopped

Cooked egg noodles – 8 oz.

Scallions – 4, chopped

Salt and pepper to taste

Directions:

Put the water, onion, celery, carrots, salt, pepper, and turkey pieces into the Instant Pot. Cover and cook on Soup function, on High for 35 minutes.

Do a natural release and open. Strain the broth and put it back into the pot.

Add the shredded turkey, carrots, and celery. Press Sauté and boil the soup.

Add the cooked noodles and cook for 1 minute more.

Serve with scallions garnishing.

Nutrition:

Calories – 458

Protein – 76.7 g.

Fat – 11.6 g.

Carbs – 9.4 g.

Crunchy Japanese Chicken Chop with Katsu Sauce

Preparation Time: 10 minutes

Cooking Time: 30 minutes

Servings: 4

Ingredients:

1 lb. boneless skinless chicken breast, sliced in half

2 large eggs

1½ cups panko bread crumbs

Salt and ground black pepper to taste

Katsu Sauce:

½ cup ketchup

2 teaspoons Worcestershire sauce

2 tablespoons soy sauce

1 tablespoon sherry

1 tablespoon brown sugar

1 teaspoon garlic, minced

Cooking spray

Directions:

In a bowl, whisk the eggs. On a plate, pour the bread crumbs.

Put the chicken on a clean surface, and dust with salt and pepper. Dip the chicken pieces in the whisked eggs first, then in bread crumbs to coat well.

Spray the basket of the air fryer with cooking spray, then arrange the breaded chicken pieces in the basket.

Put the air fry lid on and cook in the preheated instant pot at 350°F for 18 minutes or your instant-read thermometer inserted the center registers at least 165°F. Drizzle the chicken with cooking spray and flip the chicken pieces when the lid screen indicates 'TURN FOOD' halfway through.

Meanwhile, to make the katsu sauce, in a bowl, mix the ketchup, Worcestershire sauce, soy sauce, sherry, brown sugar, and garlic together. Set aside until ready to serve. Remove the chicken from the basket to a platter. Slice into strips and serve with the katsu sauce.

Nutrition:

Calories – 318

Protein – 32 g.

Fat – 6.7 g.

Carbs – 41.2 g.

Sweet and Spicy Coconut Chicken with Thai Sauce

Preparation Time: 5 minutes

Cooking Time: 15 minutes

Servings: 4

Ingredients:

½ cup canned coconut milk

1 cup sweetened coconut, shredded

1 lb.boneless skinless chicken breasts, cut to strips

½ cup pineapple juice

2 tablespoons brown sugar

1 teaspoon ground ginger

1 tablespoon soy sauce

2 teaspoons Sriracha sauce

2 eggs

1 cup panko bread crumbs

½ teaspoon ground black pepper

1½ teaspoons salt

Cooking spray

Directions:

In a bowl, mix the pineapple juice and coconut milk. Mix in the brown sugar, ginger, soy sauce, and Sriracha sauce, then add the chicken strips. Cover the dish in cling wrap and refrigerate for no less than 2 hours or overnight. and Before coating, take the chicken strips out of the refrigerator, shake off the excess.

In a bowl, whisk the eggs. In another bowl, combine the shredded coconut, bread crumbs, pepper, and salt.

Steep the chicken strips in the beaten eggs, then in the coconut mixture, and back into the the beaten egg, and again in coconut mixture.

Spray the air fryer basket with cooking spray. Place the breaded chicken strips in the basket.

Put the air fry lid on. Cook in the preheated instant pot at 375°F for 12 minutes, flipping the chicken strips when the lid screen indicates 'TURN FOOD' halfway through or until lightly browned.

Remove the chicken from the basket to a platter and serve warm.

Nutrition:

Calories – 418

Protein – 31.1 g.

Fat – 17.4 g.

Carbs – 41.1 g.

Crispy Panko Crusted Chicken Balls

Preparation Time: 15 minutes

Cooking Time: 40 minutes

Servings: 6

Ingredients:

1 package (19-ounce) ground chicken breast

1 cup panko bread crumbs

½ cup unsalted butter, softened

2 cloves garlic, crushed

2 tablespoons flat-leaf parsley, chopped

2 eggs

1 teaspoon paprika

Salt and ground black pepper, to taste

Cooking spray

Directions:

In a bowl, mix the parsley and garlic with butter. Divide and spoon 12 equal parts of the mixture on a baking sheet. Refrigerate for 20 minutes or until frozen.

Divide the ground chicken into 12 equal sized parts, and press the center of each part to make an indention. Add a spoon of butter mixture into the indention. Wrap the mixture in the ground chicken part and shape it into a ball. Repeat with remaining butter mixture and ground chicken parts. Set aside.

Whisk the eggs in a separate bowl. In a third bowl, mix the panko, paprika, black pepper, and salt.

Drop each chicken ball in the whisked eggs, then in the panko mixture. Repeat the dredging process for one more time. Shake the excess off. Transfer all balls to a baking sheet; refrigerate for 10 minutes.

Spray the air fryer basket with cooking spray, put the balls in the basket. You may need to work in batches to avoid overcrowding.

Put the air fryer lid on and cook in the preheated instant pot at 400°F for 10 minutes. Spritz the balls with cooking spray and turn the balls over when the lid screen indicates 'TURN FOOD' halfway through the cooking time.

Remove the chicken balls from the basket. Serve warm with ketchup, if desired.

Nutrition:

Calories – 154,Protein – 12.6 g., Fat – 9.4 g.

Carbs – 6.7 g.

Bang Bang Chicken with Yogurt Sauce

Preparation Time: 10 minutes

Cooking Time: 20 minutes

Servings: 4

Ingredients:

1 egg

½ cup milk

1 lb. boneless, skinless chicken breasts, cut to bite-size pieces

1 tablespoon hot pepper sauce

½ cup flour

½ cup tapioca starch

1 teaspoon garlic, granulated

½ teaspoon cumin

1½ teaspoons salt

Cooking spray

Yogurt Sauce:

¼ cup plain Greek yogurt

1 teaspoon hot sauce

3 tablespoons sweet chili sauce

Directions:

In a bowl, mix the egg, milk, and hot sauce together. In another bowl, mix the tapioca starch, flour, garlic, cumin, and salt. Set aside.

Dip the chicken pieces in the egg mixture first, then in the flour mixture. Shake off the excess.

Spray the air fryer basket with cooking spray. Arrange them in the basket, and spritz with cooking spray.

Put the air fry lid on. Cook in the preheated instant pot at 375°F for 5 minutes, shaking the basket once halfway through or until the chicken is crisp outside and juicy inside.

For the meantime, to make the yogurt sauce, in a small bowl, mix the Greek yogurt, hot sauce, and sweet chili sauce.

Take out the chicken from the basket and serve with the yogurt sauce on a plate.

Nutrition:

Calories – 313

Protein – 28.7 g.

Fat – 6.1 g.

Carbs – 34.4 g.

Mexican Marinated Turkey Fajitas

Preparation Time: 10 minutes

Cooking Time: 20 minutes

Servings: 6

Ingredients:

1 pound skinless, boneless turkey breast, cut into ½-inch thick slices

1 tablespoon chili powder

1 teaspoon garlic powder

½ teaspoon onion powder

1 tablespoon ground cumin

½ tablespoon paprika

1 teaspoon freshly ground black pepper

½ tablespoon dried Mexican oregano

2 limes, divided

1½ tablespoons vegetable oil, divided

1 large red bell pepper, julienned

1 medium yellow bell pepper, julienned

1 large red onion, halved and sliced into strips

1 jalapeño pepper, deseeded and chopped, or more to taste

¼ cup fresh cilantro, chopped

Directions:

In a bowl, mix the garlic powder, chili powder, onion powder, cumin, paprika, pepper, and oregano. Set aside. Mist the lime juice over the turkey slices in a separate large bowl, add the seasoning mixture and 1 tablespoon of oil. Toss to coat well. Set aside.

In a third bowl, put the bell peppers and onion. Drizzle with the remaining oil. Toss to fully coat. Arrange the bell peppers and onion in the air fryer basket.

Put the air fry lid on. Cook in the preheated instant pot at 375°F for 10 minutes. Shake the basket when the lid indicates 'TURN FOOD' halfway through the cooking. Add the jalapeños and cook for 5 minutes more.

Put the turkey slices over the vegetables. Cook for 7 to 8 minutes. Flip the chicken halfway through and cook until the the strips are crispy outside and the peppers are tender.

Remove the chicken and vegetables from the basket. Serve with cilantro and squeeze juice of remaining lime over.

Nutrition:

Calories – 246

Protein – 32 g.

Fat – 7 g.

Carbs –15.3 g.

Air-fried Chicken Kiev

Preparation Time: 10 minutes

Cooking Time: 30 minutes

Servings: 2

Ingredients:

2 (8-ounce) skinless, boneless chicken breast halves made into ¼ thickness

4 tablespoons butter, softened

1 clove garlic, minced

2 tablespoons fresh flat-leaf parsley, chopped

1 teaspoon salt

Salt and ground black pepper to taste

½ cup all-purpose flour

1 egg, beaten

1 cup panko bread crumbs

1 teaspoon paprika

Cooking spray

Directions:

In a bowl, evenly combine the butter, garlic, parsley, and salt. Half the butter mixture and place on a baking sheet to cool for 10 minutes.

On a clean work surface, season the chicken with salt and pepper. Place the halved butter in the center of each chicken breast. Roll the side up to wrap the butter mixture, then wrap them in plastic. Refrigerate for 30 minutes.

In another bowl, combine the flour and beaten egg. In a third bowl, combine the bread crumbs and paprika. Remove the chicken from the refrigerator. Dredge each chicken breast in the second bowl, then in the third bowl. Shower the air fryer basket with cooking spray, arrange the breaded chicken in the basket.

Put the air fry lid on and cook in the preheated instant pot at 400°F for 10 minutes. Spritz the chicken with cooking spray and flip when the lid screen indicates 'TURN FOOD' halfway through.

Take the cooked chicken to a platter and chill for 5 minutes. Slice to serve.

Nutrition:

Calories – 782

Protein – 63.5 g.

Fat – 35.1 g.

Carbs – 63.7 g.

Pretzel Crusted Chicken Chunks

Preparation Time: 5 minutes

Cooking Time: 15 minutes

Servings: 6

Ingredients:

1½ pound chicken breasts, boneless, skinless, cut into bite-sized chunks

½ cup crushed pretzels

2 eggs

1 teaspoon paprika

1 teaspoon shallot powder

Sea salt and black pepper, to taste

½ cup vegetable broth

3 tablespoons tomato paste

3 tablespoons Worcestershire sauce

1 tablespoon apple cider vinegar

1 tablespoon cornstarch

2 tablespoons olive oil

1 jalapeño pepper, minced

2 garlic cloves, chopped

1 teaspoon yellow mustard

Directions:

In a bowl, whip the eggs until frothy and dredge the chicken chunks in it until well coated.

Mix the crushed pretzels, paprika, shallot powder, salt, and pepper well in another bowl. And then toss the chicken into the mixture to get a good coating.

Arrange the well-coated chunks in the air fryer basket. Put the air fryer lid on and cook in the preheated instant pot at 375°F for 12 minutes, shaking the air fryer basket when it shows 'TURN FOOD' on the lid screen during cooking time.

In the meantime, in a third bowl combine the vegetable broth with tomato paste, Worcestershire sauce, apple cider vinegar, and cornstarch.

Heat a frying pan over medium-high heat. Add the olive oil, then stir in the jalapeño pepper and garlic, and stir-fry for 30 to 40 seconds.

Transfer the cornstarch mixture in the pan and bring it to a simmer. Keep stirring. When the sauce starts to thicken, put the air-fired chicken chunks and mustard in. Simmer it for an additional 2 minutes.

Transfer them onto a platter and serve. Bon appetit !

Nutrition:

Calories – 356,Protein – 28.2 g., Fat – 17.7 g.

Carbs – 20.4 g.

Asian Flavor Sticky Chicken Thighs

Preparation Time: 10 minutes

Cooking Time: 25 minutes

Servings: 6

Ingredients:

2 pounds chicken thighs

1 tablespoon sesame oil

¼ teaspoon paprika

1 teaspoon Chinese Five-spice powder

1 teaspoon pink Himalayan salt

1 tablespoon mustard

1 tablespoon sweet chili sauce

1 tablespoon rice wine vinegar

2 tablespoons soy sauce

6 tablespoons honey

Directions:

Rub the chicken thighs with sesame oil on all sides.

Sprinkle the paprika, Chinese Five-spice powder, and salt over to season.

Place the chicken thighs into the air fryer basket. Put the air fryer lid on and cook the thighs in batches in the preheated instant pot at 350°F for 23 minutes. Flip the thighs when the lid screen indicates 'TURN FOOD' halfway through.

For the meantime, warm up a pan over medium-high heat, and mix-in the remaining ingredients. Stir the sauce until it reduces by one-third.

Put the thighs in the pan, stir carefully until the thighs are coated with the sauce.

Transfer them to a platter. Let stand for 10 minutes. Slice to serve.

Nutrition:

Calories – 278

Protein – 27.8 g.

Fat – 10.2 g.

Carbs – 18 g.

Rustic Drumsticks with Tamari and Hot Sauce

Preparation Time: 10 minutes

Cooking Time: 30 minutes

Servings: 6

Ingredients:

6 chicken drumsticks

Nonstick cooking spray

Sauce:

½ teaspoon dried oregano

3 tablespoons tamari sauce

1 teaspoon dried thyme

6 ounces hot sauce

Directions:

Spritz the air fryer basket with the nonstick cooking spray.

Place the chicken drumsticks in the air fryer basket.

Put the air fryer lid on and cook in the preheated instant pot at 375°F for 35 minutes. Spritz the drumsticks with the nonstick cooking spray and flip when the lid screen indicates 'TURN FOOD' halfway through cooking time.

Meanwhile, warm a saucepan over medium-low heat, then add oregano, tamari sauce, thyme, and hot sauce. Cook for 2 to 4 minutes until it has a thick consistency.

Transfer the cooked drumsticks to a plate. Top with the sauce and serve.

Nutrition:

Calories – 281

Protein – 24.2 g.

Fat – 18.8 g.

Carbs – 2.7 g.

Crispy Chicken Tenders

Preparation Time: 5 minutes

Cooking Time: 20 minutes

Servings: 4

Ingredients:

1 pounds chicken tenders

2 tablespoons peanut oil

1 egg

½ cup tortilla chips, crushed

½ teaspoon garlic powder

1 teaspoon red pepper flakes

Sea salt and black pepper, to taste

2 tablespoons peanuts, roasted and roughly chopped

Cooking spray

Directions:

In a shallow bowl, beat egg. Fully mix the crushed chips, garlic powder, red pepper flakes, salt, and pepper in a separate bowl.

Brush the peanut oil all over the chicken tenders. Soak the chicken tenders in the egg mixture, then in the chip mixture. Shake off the excess.

Grease the basket with cooking spray. Arrange the tenders in the basket.

Put the air fryer lid on and cook in batches in the preheated instant pot at 350°F for 12-13 minutes until cooked through. Spritz the tenders with cooking spray and flip when the lid screen indicates 'TURN FOOD' halfway through the cooking time.

Remove the tenders from the basket to a plate and serve garnished with peanuts.

Nutrition:

Calories – 342

Protein – 36.7 g.

Fat – 16.5 g.

Carbs – 10.5 g.

Turkey Tenders with Baby Potatoes

Preparation Time: 10 minutes

Cooking Time: 40 minutes

Servings: 6

Ingredients:

2 pounds turkey tenders

1 pound baby potatoes, rubbed

2 teaspoons olive oil

1 teaspoon smoked paprika

Salt and ground black pepper, to taste

1 tablespoon fresh eavtarragon les, chopped

2 tablespoons dry white wine

Directions:

In a bowl, rub 1 teaspoon of olive oil all over the turkey tenders and sprinkle the paprika, salt, and black pepper to season.

Pour the white wine on the tenders and top with tarragon. Wrap in plastic and refrigerate to marinate for half an hour.

Arrange the tenders in the basket. Put the air fryer lid on and cook in the preheated instant pot at 350°F for 30 minutes. Turn the tenders over when it shows 'TURN FOOD' on the lid screen halfway through.

Remove tenders from the air fryer basket to a plate. Cool for 5 to 9 minutes.

Spray the remaining olive oil on the sides and bottom of the air fryer basket and cook the baby potatoes at 375°F for 16 minutes. Shake the basket for at least three times during the cooking.

Slice the turkey tenders to serve, with the baby potatoes.

Nutrition:

Calories – 316

Protein – 45.8 g.

Fat – 7.5 g.

Carbs – 14.3 g.

Mediterranean Chicken Breasts with Tomatoes

Preparation Time: 15 minutes

Cooking Time: 45 minutes

Servings: 4

Ingredients:

4 chicken breasts, bone-in

2 teaspoons olive oil

½ teaspoon salt

½ teaspoon black pepper, freshly ground

1 teaspoon cayenne pepper

1 teaspoon fresh basil, minced

1 teaspoon fresh rosemary, minced

2 tablespoons fresh parsley, minced

4 medium-sized Roma tomatoes, halved

Directions:

In a large bowl, put the rosemary, basil, parsley, cayenne pepper, salt, and black pepper, stir to mix well. Place the chicken in the bowl, toss to coat well.

Rub 1 teaspoon of olive oil all over the air fryer basket, then arrange the chicken into the basket.

Put the air fryer lid on and cook in batches in the preheat instant pot at 375°F for 16 minutes until the breasts are golden brown. Flip the breasts when the lid screen indicates 'TURN FOOD' halfway through cooking time. Remove the chicken from the basket to a dish, and place the halved tomatoes in the air fryer basket. Drizzle with the remaining olive oil. Sprinkle the sea salt to season. Cook the halved tomatoes at 350°F for about 10 minutes, shaking the basket once when it shows 'TURN FOOD' on the lid screen during cooking time.

Serve chicken breasts with tomatoes.

Nutrition:

Calories – 316

Protein – 37 g.

Fat – 17.2 g.

Carbs – 2.8 g.

Spicy Thai Duck Breasts with Candy Onion

Preparation Time: 10 minutes

Cooking Time: 30 minutes

Servings: 4

Ingredients:

1½ pounds duck breasts, skin removed

1 cup candy onions, halved

½ teaspoon smoked paprika

1 tablespoon Thai red curry paste

⅓ teaspoon black pepper

½ teaspoon cayenne pepper

1 teaspoon kosher salt

¼ small pack coriander, chopped

Directions:

On a clean work surface, flatten the duck into 1-inch thick with a rolling pin. Rub paprika, red curry paste, black pepper, cayenne pepper, and kosher salt on the duck breasts.

Use 2 sheets of foil to wrap the duck breasts, then arrange in the air fryer basket.

Put the air fryer lid on and cook in the preheated instant pot at 375°F for 33 to 35 minutes. Top them with halved candy onions halfway through the cooking time. Transfer the cooked duck to a platter. Sprinkle with coriander to serve.

Nutrition:

Calories – 363

Protein – 42.4 g.

Fat – 18.8 g.

Carbs – 5 g.

Homemade Chicken Legs with Turnip

Preparation Time: 10 minutes

Cooking Time: 20 minutes

Servings: 3

Ingredients:

1 pound chicken legs

1 turnip, trimmed and sliced

1 teaspoon paprika

½ teaspoon ground black pepper

1 teaspoon Himalayan salt

1 teaspoon butter, melted

Nonstick cooking spray

Directions:

Use the nonstick cooking spray to coat the sides and bottom of the air fryer basket.

On a clean work surface, sprinkle paprika, ground black pepper, and salt on the chicken legs to season.

Arrange the chicken legs in the air fryer basket. Put the air fryer lid on and cook in the preheated instant pot at 375°F for 10 minutes. Flip the legs when the lid screen indicates 'TURN FOOD' halfway through.

Drizzle the melted butter on the turnip slices and place them in the basket.

Close it and cook the turnip with the chicken at 375°F for another 15 minutes. Flip the chicken legs and turnip when the lid screen indicates 'TURN FOOD'.

Transfer to a platter and serve.

Nutrition:

Calories – 206

Protein – 29.6 g.

Fat – 7.9 g.

Carbs – 3.5 g.

Crunchy Chicken Drumettes

Preparation Time: 10 minutes

Cooking Time: 20 minutes

Servings: 3

Ingredients:

6 chicken drumettes

⅓ cup all-purpose flour

1 teaspoon sea salt

1 teaspoon garlic paste

1 teaspoon dried rosemary

½ teaspoon ground white pepper

1 egg

1 heaping tablespoon fresh chives, chopped

Nonstick cooking spray

Directions:

In a bowl, mix the garlic paste, flour, salt, rosemary and white pepper together. Whisk the eggs until frothy in a separate bowl.

Dredge the chicken drumettes in the flour mixture, and in the whisked eggs, and the flour mixture again.

Use the nonstick cooking spray to lightly coat the bottom and sides of the air fryer basket.

Arrange the coated chicken drumettes in the air fryer basket. Put the air fryer lid on and cook in the preheated instant pot at 375°F for 22 minutes.

Transfer to a serving dish, let stand, top with chives to serve.

Nutrition:

Calories – 346

Protein – 42 g.

Fat – 9.2 g.

Carbs – 11.4 g.

Chicken Casserole

Preparation Time: 10 minutes

Cooking Time: 20 minutes

Servings: 2

Ingredients:

Pepperoni – 8 slices, uncured

Mozzarella cheese – ½ cup, shredded

Full-fat cheddar cheese – ½ cup, shredded

Chicken – ½ pound, ground

Egg – 1

Garlic – ½ tsp. minced

Full-fat Parmesan cheese – ¼ cup, grated

Dried parsley – ¼ tsp.

Thyme – ¼ tsp.

Dried basil – ¼ tsp.

Black pepper – ¼ tsp.

Crushed red pepper – ¼ tsp.

Dried oregano – ¼ tsp.

Fire-roasted tomatoes – 7 ounces

Water – 1 cup for the pot

Directions:

Add 1-cup water into the Instant Pot.

Insert the trivet.

In a bowl, combine tomatoes, oregano, red pepper, black pepper, basil, thyme, parsley, Parmesan, garlic, egg, chicken, cheddar, mozzarella, and pepperoni slices.

Blend well and put the mixture into a greased dish.

Place the dish on top of the stand.

Use an aluminum foil to cover loosely.

Make sure to lock the lid and cook 20 minutes on High.

Do a natural release and open.

Serve.

Nutrition:

Calories – 538

Protein – 57.9 g.

Fat – 30.8 g.

Carbs – 4.9 g.

Broccoli Chicken Casserole

Preparation Time: 15 minutes

Cooking Time: 15 minutes

Servings: 2

Ingredients:

Broccoli florets – ½ cup

Fresh spinach – ¼ cup

Whole-milk ricotta – 2 Tbsp.

Alfredo sauce – ¾ cup

Salt – ¼ tsp.

Pepper to taste

Thin-sliced deli chicken – ½ pound

Whole-milk mozzarella cheese – ½ cup, shredded

Water – ½ cup for the pot

Directions:

Place broccoli in a bowl.

Add salt, pepper, sauce, ricotta, and spinach and mix.

Separate into sections with a spoon.

Layer chicken in a bowl. Top the chicken with veggie mix.

Then top veggie with mozzarella. Repeat until all veggie mix is used.

Finish casserole with mozzarella and cover the dish with foil.

Empty water to the Instant Pot and place steamer rack in the pot.

Put the dish on top of the rack. Close the lid.

Cook on High for 15 minutes.

Do a quick release and remove it.

You can broil in the oven for a few minutes to make the top golden.

Nutrition:

Calories – 283

Protein – 29.3 g.

Fat – 13.3 g.

Carbs – 9.1 g.

Oregano Chicken

Preparation Time: 10 minutes

Cooking Time: 20 minutes

Servings: 4

Ingredients:

2 chicken breasts, skinless, boneless and cubed

1 cup tomato passata

½ cup chicken stock

1 tablespoon oregano, chopped

A pinch of salt and black pepper

1 teaspoon sweet paprika

1 tablespoon cilantro, chopped

Directions:

In your instant pot, combine all ingredients, toss, and Make sure to lock the lid and cook on High for 20 minutes.

Naturally release the pressure for 10 minutes, divide the mix between plates and serve.

Nutrition:

Calories – 183

Protein – 13.4 g.

Fat – 2.5 g.

Carbs – 1.5 g.

Spiced Chicken Bites

Preparation Time: 10 minutes

Cooking Time: 24 minutes

Servings: 4

Ingredients:

2 chicken breasts, skinless, boneless and cubed

2 tablespoons avocado oil

½ teaspoon turmeric powder

½ teaspoon cumin, ground

½ teaspoon allspice, ground

½ teaspoon cinnamon powder

1 teaspoon sweet paprika

2 tablespoons tomato paste

1 cup chicken stock

Directions:

Put your instant pot on Sauté mode, add the oil, heat it up, add the chicken and let it cook for 2 minutes on each side.
Add remaining ingredients, close the pot and cook on High for 20 minutes
Naturally release the pressure for 10 minutes, divide the mix between plates and serve.

Nutrition:

Calories – 238

Protein – 33.3 g.

Fat – 9.7 g.

Carbs – 2.9 g.

Conclusion

When you are on a diet trying to lose weight or manage a condition, you will be strictly confined to follow an eating plan. Such plans often place numerous demands on individuals: food may need to be boiled, other foods are forbidden, permitting you only to eat small portions and so on.

On the other hand, a lifestyle such as the Mediterranean diet is entirely stress-free. It is easy to follow because there are almost no restrictions. There is no time limit on the Mediterranean diet because it is more of a lifestyle than a diet. You do not need to stop at some point but carry on for the rest of your life. The foods that you eat under the Mediterranean model include unrefined cereals, white meats, and the occasional dairy products.

The Mediterranean lifestyle, unlike other diets, also requires you to engage with family and friends and share meals together. It has been noted that communities around the Mediterranean spend between one and two hours enjoying their meals. This kind of bonding between family members or friends helps bring people closer together, which helps foster closer bonds hence fewer cases of depression, loneliness, or stress, all of which are precursors to chronic diseases.

You will achieve many benefits using the Instant Pot Pressure Cooker. These are just a few instances you will discover in your Mediterranean-style recipes:

Pressure cooking means that you can (on average) cook meals 75% faster than boiling/braising on the stovetop or baking and roasting in a conventional oven.

This is especially helpful for vegan meals that entail the use of dried beans, legumes, and pulses. Instead of pre-soaking these ingredients for hours before use, you can pour them directly into the Instant Pot, add water, and pressure cook these for several minutes. However, always follow your recipe carefully since they have been tested for accuracy.

Nutrients are preserved. You can use your pressure-cooking techniques using the Instant Pot to ensure the heat is evenly and quickly distributed. It is not essential to immerse the food into the water. You will provide plenty of water in the cooker for efficient steaming. You will also be saving the essential vitamins and minerals. The food won't become oxidized by the exposure of air or heat. Enjoy those fresh green veggies with their natural and vibrant colors.

The cooking elements help keep the foods fully sealed, so the steam and aromas don't linger throughout your entire home. That is a plus, especially for items such as cabbage, which throws out a distinctive smell.

You will find that beans and whole grains will have a softer texture and will have an improved taste. The meal will be cooked consistently since the Instant Pot provides even heat distribution.

You'll also save tons of time and money. You will be using much less water, and the pot is fully insulated, making it more energy-efficient when compared to boiling or steaming your foods on the stovetop. It is also less expensive than using a microwave, not to mention how much more flavorful the food will be when prepared in the Instant Pot cooker.

You can delay the cooking of your food items so you can plan ahead of time. You won't need to stand around as you await your meal. You can reduce the cooking time by reducing the 'hands-on' time. Just leave for work or a day of activities, and you will come home to a special treat.

In a nutshell, the Instant Pot is:

Easy To Use Healthy recipes for the entire family are provided.

You can make authentic one-pot recipes in your Instant Pot.

If you forget to switch on your slow cooker, you can make any meal done in a few minutes in your Instant Pot.

You can securely and smoothly cook meat from frozen.

It's a laid-back way to cook. You don't have to watch a pan on the stove or a pot in the oven.

The pressure cooking procedure develops delicious flavors swiftly.

Lightning Source UK Ltd.
Milton Keynes UK
UKHW021821160421
382091UK00005B/76